My Stitching Friends

Address Book For My Needlework Friends & Social Media Contacts

Name

Social Media Handle

Mailing Address

Email Address

YouTube Channel

Instagram

Facebook

Streaming

Website

Blog

Birthday or important date(s):

How we met:

Favorite Stitching Things:

Fun Friend Facts:

Name

Social Media Handle

Mailing Address

Email Address

YouTube Channel

Instagram

Facebook

Streaming

Website

Blog

Birthday or important date(s):

How we met:

Favorite Stitching Things:

Fun Friend Facts:

Name

Social Media Handle

Mailing Address

Email Address

YouTube Channel

Instagram

Facebook

Streaming

Website

Blog

Birthday or important date(s):

How we met:

Favorite Stitching Things:

Fun Friend Facts:

Name

Social Media Handle

Mailing Address

Email Address

YouTube Channel

Instagram

Facebook

Streaming

Website

Blog

Birthday or important date(s):

How we met:

Favorite Stitching Things:

Fun Friend Facts:

Name
Social Media Handle
Mailing Address

Email Address
YouTube Channel
Instagram
Facebook
Streaming
Website
Blog
Birthday or important date(s):

How we met:

Favorite Stitching Things:

Fun Friend Facts:

Name
Social Media Handle
Mailing Address

Email Address
YouTube Channel
Instagram
Facebook
Streaming
Website
Blog
Birthday or important date(s):

How we met:

Favorite Stitching Things:

Fun Friend Facts:

Name

Social Media Handle

Mailing Address

Email Address

YouTube Channel

Instagram

Facebook

Streaming

Website

Blog

Birthday or important date(s):

How we met:

Favorite Stitching Things:

Fun Friend Facts:

Name

Social Media Handle

Mailing Address

Email Address

YouTube Channel

Instagram

Facebook

Streaming

Website

Blog

Birthday or important date(s):

How we met:

Favorite Stitching Things:

Fun Friend Facts:

Name
Social Media Handle
Mailing Address

Email Address
YouTube Channel
Instagram
Facebook
Streaming
Website
Blog
Birthday or important date(s):

How we met:

Favorite Stitching Things:

Fun Friend Facts:

Name
Social Media Handle
Mailing Address

Email Address
YouTube Channel
Instagram
Facebook
Streaming
Website
Blog
Birthday or important date(s):

How we met:

Favorite Stitching Things:

Fun Friend Facts:

Name

Social Media Handle

Mailing Address

Email Address

YouTube Channel

Instagram

Facebook

Streaming

Website

Blog

Birthday or important date(s):

How we met:

Favorite Stitching Things:

Fun Friend Facts:

Name

Social Media Handle

Mailing Address

Email Address

YouTube Channel

Instagram

Facebook

Streaming

Website

Blog

Birthday or important date(s):

How we met:

Favorite Stitching Things:

Fun Friend Facts:

Name

Social Media Handle

Mailing Address

Email Address

YouTube Channel

Instagram

Facebook

Streaming

Website

Blog

Birthday or important date(s):

How we met:

Favorite Stitching Things:

Fun Friend Facts:

Name

Social Media Handle

Mailing Address

Email Address

YouTube Channel

Instagram

Facebook

Streaming

Website

Blog

Birthday or important date(s):

How we met:

Favorite Stitching Things:

Fun Friend Facts:

Name
Social Media Handle
Mailing Address

Email Address
YouTube Channel
Instagram
Facebook
Streaming
Website
Blog
Birthday or important date(s):

How we met:

Favorite Stitching Things:

Fun Friend Facts:

Name
Social Media Handle
Mailing Address

Email Address
YouTube Channel
Instagram
Facebook
Streaming
Website
Blog
Birthday or important date(s):

How we met:

Favorite Stitching Things:

Fun Friend Facts:

Name _____
Social Media Handle _____
Mailing Address _____

Email Address _____
YouTube Channel _____
Instagram _____
Facebook _____
Streaming _____
Website _____
Blog _____
Birthday or important date(s): _____

How we met: _____

Favorite Stitching Things: _____
_____
_____

Fun Friend Facts: _____
_____
_____

Name _____
Social Media Handle _____
Mailing Address _____

Email Address _____
YouTube Channel _____
Instagram _____
Facebook _____
Streaming _____
Website _____
Blog _____
Birthday or important date(s): _____

How we met: _____

Favorite Stitching Things: _____
_____
_____

Fun Friend Facts: _____
_____
_____

Name

Social Media Handle

Mailing Address

Email Address

YouTube Channel

Instagram

Facebook

Streaming

Website

Blog

Birthday or important date(s):

How we met:

Favorite Stitching Things:

Fun Friend Facts:

Name

Social Media Handle

Mailing Address

Email Address

YouTube Channel

Instagram

Facebook

Streaming

Website

Blog

Birthday or important date(s):

How we met:

Favorite Stitching Things:

Fun Friend Facts:

Name
Social Media Handle
Mailing Address

Email Address
YouTube Channel
Instagram
Facebook
Streaming
Website
Blog
Birthday or important date(s):

How we met:

Favorite Stitching Things:

Fun Friend Facts:

Name
Social Media Handle
Mailing Address

Email Address
YouTube Channel
Instagram
Facebook
Streaming
Website
Blog
Birthday or important date(s):

How we met:

Favorite Stitching Things:

Fun Friend Facts:

Name

Social Media Handle

Mailing Address

Email Address

YouTube Channel

Instagram

Facebook

Streaming

Website

Blog

Birthday or important date(s):

How we met:

Favorite Stitching Things:

Fun Friend Facts:

Name

Social Media Handle

Mailing Address

Email Address

YouTube Channel

Instagram

Facebook

Streaming

Website

Blog

Birthday or important date(s):

How we met:

Favorite Stitching Things:

Fun Friend Facts:

Name

Social Media Handle

Mailing Address

Email Address

YouTube Channel

Instagram

Facebook

Streaming

Website

Blog

Birthday or important date(s):

How we met:

Favorite Stitching Things:

Fun Friend Facts:

Name

Social Media Handle

Mailing Address

Email Address

YouTube Channel

Instagram

Facebook

Streaming

Website

Blog

Birthday or important date(s):

How we met:

Favorite Stitching Things:

Fun Friend Facts:

Name
Social Media Handle
Mailing Address

Email Address
YouTube Channel
Instagram
Facebook
Streaming
Website
Blog
Birthday or important date(s):

How we met:

Favorite Stitching Things:

Fun Friend Facts:

Name
Social Media Handle
Mailing Address

Email Address
YouTube Channel
Instagram
Facebook
Streaming
Website
Blog
Birthday or important date(s):

How we met:

Favorite Stitching Things:

Fun Friend Facts:

Name
Social Media Handle
Mailing Address

Email Address
YouTube Channel
Instagram
Facebook
Streaming
Website
Blog
Birthday or important date(s):

How we met:

Favorite Stitching Things:

Fun Friend Facts:

Name
Social Media Handle
Mailing Address

Email Address
YouTube Channel
Instagram
Facebook
Streaming
Website
Blog
Birthday or important date(s):

How we met:

Favorite Stitching Things:

Fun Friend Facts:

Name

Social Media Handle

Mailing Address

Email Address

YouTube Channel

Instagram

Facebook

Streaming

Website

Blog

Birthday or important date(s):

How we met:

Favorite Stitching Things:

Fun Friend Facts:

Name

Social Media Handle

Mailing Address

Email Address

YouTube Channel

Instagram

Facebook

Streaming

Website

Blog

Birthday or important date(s):

How we met:

Favorite Stitching Things:

Fun Friend Facts:

Name
Social Media Handle
Mailing Address

Email Address
YouTube Channel
Instagram
Facebook
Streaming
Website
Blog
Birthday or important date(s):

How we met:

Favorite Stitching Things:

Fun Friend Facts:

Name
Social Media Handle
Mailing Address

Email Address
YouTube Channel
Instagram
Facebook
Streaming
Website
Blog
Birthday or important date(s):

How we met:

Favorite Stitching Things:

Fun Friend Facts:

Name
Social Media Handle
Mailing Address

Email Address
YouTube Channel
Instagram
Facebook
Streaming
Website
Blog
Birthday or important date(s):

How we met:

Favorite Stitching Things:

Fun Friend Facts:

Name
Social Media Handle
Mailing Address

Email Address
YouTube Channel
Instagram
Facebook
Streaming
Website
Blog
Birthday or important date(s):

How we met:

Favorite Stitching Things:

Fun Friend Facts:

Name _____
Social Media Handle _____
Mailing Address _____
_____
Email Address _____
YouTube Channel _____
Instagram _____
Facebook _____
Streaming _____
Website _____
Blog _____
Birthday or important date(s): _____

How we met: _____
_____
Favorite Stitching Things: _____
_____
_____
Fun Friend Facts: _____
_____
_____
_____

Name _____
Social Media Handle _____
Mailing Address _____
_____
Email Address _____
YouTube Channel _____
Instagram _____
Facebook _____
Streaming _____
Website _____
Blog _____
Birthday or important date(s): _____

How we met: _____
_____
Favorite Stitching Things: _____
_____
_____
Fun Friend Facts: _____
_____
_____
_____

Name

Social Media Handle

Mailing Address

Email Address

YouTube Channel

Instagram

Facebook

Streaming

Website

Blog

Birthday or important date(s):

How we met:

Favorite Stitching Things:

Fun Friend Facts:

Name

Social Media Handle

Mailing Address

Email Address

YouTube Channel

Instagram

Facebook

Streaming

Website

Blog

Birthday or important date(s):

How we met:

Favorite Stitching Things:

Fun Friend Facts:

Name
Social Media Handle
Mailing Address

Email Address
YouTube Channel
Instagram
Facebook
Streaming
Website
Blog
Birthday or important date(s):

How we met:

Favorite Stitching Things:

Fun Friend Facts:

Name
Social Media Handle
Mailing Address

Email Address
YouTube Channel
Instagram
Facebook
Streaming
Website
Blog
Birthday or important date(s):

How we met:

Favorite Stitching Things:

Fun Friend Facts:

Name

Social Media Handle

Mailing Address

Email Address

YouTube Channel

Instagram

Facebook

Streaming

Website

Blog

Birthday or important date(s):

How we met:

Favorite Stitching Things:

Fun Friend Facts:

Name

Social Media Handle

Mailing Address

Email Address

YouTube Channel

Instagram

Facebook

Streaming

Website

Blog

Birthday or important date(s):

How we met:

Favorite Stitching Things:

Fun Friend Facts:

Name
Social Media Handle
Mailing Address

Email Address
YouTube Channel
Instagram
Facebook
Streaming
Website
Blog
Birthday or important date(s):

How we met:

Favorite Stitching Things:

Fun Friend Facts:

Name
Social Media Handle
Mailing Address

Email Address
YouTube Channel
Instagram
Facebook
Streaming
Website
Blog
Birthday or important date(s):

How we met:

Favorite Stitching Things:

Fun Friend Facts:

Name
Social Media Handle
Mailing Address

Email Address
YouTube Channel
Instagram
Facebook
Streaming
Website
Blog
Birthday or important date(s):

How we met:

Favorite Stitching Things:

Fun Friend Facts:

Name
Social Media Handle
Mailing Address

Email Address
YouTube Channel
Instagram
Facebook
Streaming
Website
Blog
Birthday or important date(s):

How we met:

Favorite Stitching Things:

Fun Friend Facts:

Name

Social Media Handle

Mailing Address

Email Address

YouTube Channel

Instagram

Facebook

Streaming

Website

Blog

Birthday or important date(s):

How we met:

Favorite Stitching Things:

Fun Friend Facts:

Name

Social Media Handle

Mailing Address

Email Address

YouTube Channel

Instagram

Facebook

Streaming

Website

Blog

Birthday or important date(s):

How we met:

Favorite Stitching Things:

Fun Friend Facts:

Name
Social Media Handle
Mailing Address

Email Address
YouTube Channel
Instagram
Facebook
Streaming
Website
Blog
Birthday or important date(s):

How we met:

Favorite Stitching Things:

Fun Friend Facts:

Name
Social Media Handle
Mailing Address

Email Address
YouTube Channel
Instagram
Facebook
Streaming
Website
Blog
Birthday or important date(s):

How we met:

Favorite Stitching Things:

Fun Friend Facts:

Name
Social Media Handle
Mailing Address

Email Address
YouTube Channel
Instagram
Facebook
Streaming
Website
Blog
Birthday or important date(s):

How we met:

Favorite Stitching Things:

Fun Friend Facts:

Name
Social Media Handle
Mailing Address

Email Address
YouTube Channel
Instagram
Facebook
Streaming
Website
Blog
Birthday or important date(s):

How we met:

Favorite Stitching Things:

Fun Friend Facts:

Name _____

Social Media Handle _____

Mailing Address _____
_____

Email Address _____

YouTube Channel _____

Instagram _____

Facebook _____

Streaming _____

Website _____

Blog _____

Birthday or important date(s): _____
_____

How we met: _____
_____

Favorite Stitching Things: _____
_____

Fun Friend Facts: _____
_____
_____

Name _____

Social Media Handle _____

Mailing Address _____
_____

Email Address _____

YouTube Channel _____

Instagram _____

Facebook _____

Streaming _____

Website _____

Blog _____

Birthday or important date(s): _____
_____

How we met: _____
_____

Favorite Stitching Things: _____
_____

Fun Friend Facts: _____
_____
_____

Name
Social Media Handle
Mailing Address

Email Address
YouTube Channel
Instagram
Facebook
Streaming
Website
Blog
Birthday or important date(s):

How we met:

Favorite Stitching Things:

Fun Friend Facts:

Name
Social Media Handle
Mailing Address

Email Address
YouTube Channel
Instagram
Facebook
Streaming
Website
Blog
Birthday or important date(s):

How we met:

Favorite Stitching Things:

Fun Friend Facts:

Name

Social Media Handle

Mailing Address

Email Address

YouTube Channel

Instagram

Facebook

Streaming

Website

Blog

Birthday or important date(s):

How we met:

Favorite Stitching Things:

Fun Friend Facts:

Name

Social Media Handle

Mailing Address

Email Address

YouTube Channel

Instagram

Facebook

Streaming

Website

Blog

Birthday or important date(s):

How we met:

Favorite Stitching Things:

Fun Friend Facts:

Name
Social Media Handle
Mailing Address

Email Address
YouTube Channel
Instagram
Facebook
Streaming
Website
Blog
Birthday or important date(s):

How we met:

Favorite Stitching Things:

Fun Friend Facts:

Name
Social Media Handle
Mailing Address

Email Address
YouTube Channel
Instagram
Facebook
Streaming
Website
Blog
Birthday or important date(s):

How we met:

Favorite Stitching Things:

Fun Friend Facts:

Name
Social Media Handle
Mailing Address

Email Address
YouTube Channel
Instagram
Facebook
Streaming
Website
Blog
Birthday or important date(s):

How we met:

Favorite Stitching Things:

Fun Friend Facts:

Name
Social Media Handle
Mailing Address

Email Address
YouTube Channel
Instagram
Facebook
Streaming
Website
Blog
Birthday or important date(s):

How we met:

Favorite Stitching Things:

Fun Friend Facts:

Name
Social Media Handle
Mailing Address

Email Address
YouTube Channel
Instagram
Facebook
Streaming
Website
Blog
Birthday or important date(s):

How we met:

Favorite Stitching Things:

Fun Friend Facts:

Name
Social Media Handle
Mailing Address

Email Address
YouTube Channel
Instagram
Facebook
Streaming
Website
Blog
Birthday or important date(s):

How we met:

Favorite Stitching Things:

Fun Friend Facts:

Name _____
Social Media Handle _____
Mailing Address _____
_____
Email Address _____
YouTube Channel _____
Instagram _____
Facebook _____
Streaming _____
Website _____
Blog _____
Birthday or important date(s): _____
_____
How we met: _____
_____
Favorite Stitching Things: _____
_____
_____
Fun Friend Facts: _____
_____
_____
_____

Name _____
Social Media Handle _____
Mailing Address _____
_____
Email Address _____
YouTube Channel _____
Instagram _____
Facebook _____
Streaming _____
Website _____
Blog _____
Birthday or important date(s): _____
_____
How we met: _____
_____
Favorite Stitching Things: _____
_____
_____
Fun Friend Facts: _____
_____
_____
_____

Name
Social Media Handle
Mailing Address

Email Address
YouTube Channel
Instagram
Facebook
Streaming
Website
Blog
Birthday or important date(s):

How we met:

Favorite Stitching Things:

Fun Friend Facts:

Name
Social Media Handle
Mailing Address

Email Address
YouTube Channel
Instagram
Facebook
Streaming
Website
Blog
Birthday or important date(s):

How we met:

Favorite Stitching Things:

Fun Friend Facts:

Name
Social Media Handle
Mailing Address

Email Address
YouTube Channel
Instagram
Facebook
Streaming
Website
Blog
Birthday or important date(s):

How we met:

Favorite Stitching Things:

Fun Friend Facts:

Name
Social Media Handle
Mailing Address

Email Address
YouTube Channel
Instagram
Facebook
Streaming
Website
Blog
Birthday or important date(s):

How we met:

Favorite Stitching Things:

Fun Friend Facts:

Name
Social Media Handle
Mailing Address

Email Address
YouTube Channel
Instagram
Facebook
Streaming
Website
Blog
Birthday or important date(s):

How we met:

Favorite Stitching Things:

Fun Friend Facts:

Name
Social Media Handle
Mailing Address

Email Address
YouTube Channel
Instagram
Facebook
Streaming
Website
Blog
Birthday or important date(s):

How we met:

Favorite Stitching Things:

Fun Friend Facts:

Name

Social Media Handle

Mailing Address

Email Address

YouTube Channel

Instagram

Facebook

Streaming

Website

Blog

Birthday or important date(s):

How we met:

Favorite Stitching Things:

Fun Friend Facts:

Name

Social Media Handle

Mailing Address

Email Address

YouTube Channel

Instagram

Facebook

Streaming

Website

Blog

Birthday or important date(s):

How we met:

Favorite Stitching Things:

Fun Friend Facts:

Name

Social Media Handle

Mailing Address

Email Address

YouTube Channel

Instagram

Facebook

Streaming

Website

Blog

Birthday or important date(s):

How we met:

Favorite Stitching Things:

Fun Friend Facts:

Name

Social Media Handle

Mailing Address

Email Address

YouTube Channel

Instagram

Facebook

Streaming

Website

Blog

Birthday or important date(s):

How we met:

Favorite Stitching Things:

Fun Friend Facts:

Name
Social Media Handle
Mailing Address

Email Address
YouTube Channel
Instagram
Facebook
Streaming
Website
Blog
Birthday or important date(s):

How we met:

Favorite Stitching Things:

Fun Friend Facts:

Name
Social Media Handle
Mailing Address

Email Address
YouTube Channel
Instagram
Facebook
Streaming
Website
Blog
Birthday or important date(s):

How we met:

Favorite Stitching Things:

Fun Friend Facts:

Name
Social Media Handle
Mailing Address

Email Address
YouTube Channel
Instagram
Facebook
Streaming
Website
Blog
Birthday or important date(s):

How we met:

Favorite Stitching Things:

Fun Friend Facts:

Name
Social Media Handle
Mailing Address

Email Address
YouTube Channel
Instagram
Facebook
Streaming
Website
Blog
Birthday or important date(s):

How we met:

Favorite Stitching Things:

Fun Friend Facts:

Name
Social Media Handle
Mailing Address

Email Address
YouTube Channel
Instagram
Facebook
Streaming
Website
Blog
Birthday or important date(s):

How we met:

Favorite Stitching Things:

Fun Friend Facts:

Name
Social Media Handle
Mailing Address

Email Address
YouTube Channel
Instagram
Facebook
Streaming
Website
Blog
Birthday or important date(s):

How we met:

Favorite Stitching Things:

Fun Friend Facts:

Name
Social Media Handle
Mailing Address

Email Address
YouTube Channel
Instagram
Facebook
Streaming
Website
Blog
Birthday or important date(s):

How we met:

Favorite Stitching Things:

Fun Friend Facts:

Name
Social Media Handle
Mailing Address

Email Address
YouTube Channel
Instagram
Facebook
Streaming
Website
Blog
Birthday or important date(s):

How we met:

Favorite Stitching Things:

Fun Friend Facts:

Name _____
Social Media Handle _____
Mailing Address _____
_____
Email Address _____
YouTube Channel _____
Instagram _____
Facebook _____
Streaming _____
Website _____
Blog _____
Birthday or important date(s): ____
_____
How we met: _____
_____
Favorite Stitching Things: _____
_____
_____
Fun Friend Facts: _____
_____
_____
_____

Name _____
Social Media Handle _____
Mailing Address _____
_____
Email Address _____
YouTube Channel _____
Instagram _____
Facebook _____
Streaming _____
Website _____
Blog _____
Birthday or important date(s): ____
_____
How we met: _____
_____
Favorite Stitching Things: _____
_____
_____
Fun Friend Facts: _____
_____
_____
_____

Name

Social Media Handle

Mailing Address

Email Address

YouTube Channel

Instagram

Facebook

Streaming

Website

Blog

Birthday or important date(s):

How we met:

Favorite Stitching Things:

Fun Friend Facts:

Name

Social Media Handle

Mailing Address

Email Address

YouTube Channel

Instagram

Facebook

Streaming

Website

Blog

Birthday or important date(s):

How we met:

Favorite Stitching Things:

Fun Friend Facts:

Name

Social Media Handle

Mailing Address

Email Address

YouTube Channel

Instagram

Facebook

Streaming

Website

Blog

Birthday or important date(s):

How we met:

Favorite Stitching Things:

Fun Friend Facts:

Name

Social Media Handle

Mailing Address

Email Address

YouTube Channel

Instagram

Facebook

Streaming

Website

Blog

Birthday or important date(s):

How we met:

Favorite Stitching Things:

Fun Friend Facts:

Name
Social Media Handle
Mailing Address

Email Address
YouTube Channel
Instagram
Facebook
Streaming
Website
Blog
Birthday or important date(s):

How we met:

Favorite Stitching Things:

Fun Friend Facts:

Name
Social Media Handle
Mailing Address

Email Address
YouTube Channel
Instagram
Facebook
Streaming
Website
Blog
Birthday or important date(s):

How we met:

Favorite Stitching Things:

Fun Friend Facts:

Name

Social Media Handle

Mailing Address

Email Address

YouTube Channel

Instagram

Facebook

Streaming

Website

Blog

Birthday or important date(s):

How we met:

Favorite Stitching Things:

Fun Friend Facts:

Name

Social Media Handle

Mailing Address

Email Address

YouTube Channel

Instagram

Facebook

Streaming

Website

Blog

Birthday or important date(s):

How we met:

Favorite Stitching Things:

Fun Friend Facts:

Name

Social Media Handle

Mailing Address

Email Address

YouTube Channel

Instagram

Facebook

Streaming

Website

Blog

Birthday or important date(s):

How we met:

Favorite Stitching Things:

Fun Friend Facts:

Name

Social Media Handle

Mailing Address

Email Address

YouTube Channel

Instagram

Facebook

Streaming

Website

Blog

Birthday or important date(s):

How we met:

Favorite Stitching Things:

Fun Friend Facts:

Name

Social Media Handle

Mailing Address

Email Address

YouTube Channel

Instagram

Facebook

Streaming

Website

Blog

Birthday or important date(s):

How we met:

Favorite Stitching Things:

Fun Friend Facts:

Name

Social Media Handle

Mailing Address

Email Address

YouTube Channel

Instagram

Facebook

Streaming

Website

Blog

Birthday or important date(s):

How we met:

Favorite Stitching Things:

Fun Friend Facts:

Name
Social Media Handle
Mailing Address

Email Address
YouTube Channel
Instagram
Facebook
Streaming
Website
Blog
Birthday or important date(s):

How we met:

Favorite Stitching Things:

Fun Friend Facts:

Name
Social Media Handle
Mailing Address

Email Address
YouTube Channel
Instagram
Facebook
Streaming
Website
Blog
Birthday or important date(s):

How we met:

Favorite Stitching Things:

Fun Friend Facts:

Name

Social Media Handle

Mailing Address

Email Address

YouTube Channel

Instagram

Facebook

Streaming

Website

Blog

Birthday or important date(s):

How we met:

Favorite Stitching Things:

Fun Friend Facts:

Name

Social Media Handle

Mailing Address

Email Address

YouTube Channel

Instagram

Facebook

Streaming

Website

Blog

Birthday or important date(s):

How we met:

Favorite Stitching Things:

Fun Friend Facts:

Name
Social Media Handle
Mailing Address

Email Address
YouTube Channel
Instagram
Facebook
Streaming
Website
Blog
Birthday or important date(s):

How we met:

Favorite Stitching Things:

Fun Friend Facts:

Name
Social Media Handle
Mailing Address

Email Address
YouTube Channel
Instagram
Facebook
Streaming
Website
Blog
Birthday or important date(s):

How we met:

Favorite Stitching Things:

Fun Friend Facts:

Name _____
Social Media Handle _____
Mailing Address _____
_____
Email Address _____
YouTube Channel _____
Instagram _____
Facebook _____
Streaming _____
Website _____
Blog _____
Birthday or important date(s): _____
_____
How we met: _____
_____
Favorite Stitching Things: _____
_____
_____
Fun Friend Facts: _____
_____
_____
_____

Name _____
Social Media Handle _____
Mailing Address _____
_____
Email Address _____
YouTube Channel _____
Instagram _____
Facebook _____
Streaming _____
Website _____
Blog _____
Birthday or important date(s): _____
_____
How we met: _____
_____
Favorite Stitching Things: _____
_____
_____
Fun Friend Facts: _____
_____
_____
_____

Name
Social Media Handle
Mailing Address

Email Address
YouTube Channel
Instagram
Facebook
Streaming
Website
Blog
Birthday or important date(s):

How we met:

Favorite Stitching Things:

Fun Friend Facts:

Name
Social Media Handle
Mailing Address

Email Address
YouTube Channel
Instagram
Facebook
Streaming
Website
Blog
Birthday or important date(s):

How we met:

Favorite Stitching Things:

Fun Friend Facts:

Name

Social Media Handle

Mailing Address

Email Address

YouTube Channel

Instagram

Facebook

Streaming

Website

Blog

Birthday or important date(s):

How we met:

Favorite Stitching Things:

Fun Friend Facts:

Name

Social Media Handle

Mailing Address

Email Address

YouTube Channel

Instagram

Facebook

Streaming

Website

Blog

Birthday or important date(s):

How we met:

Favorite Stitching Things:

Fun Friend Facts:

Name
Social Media Handle
Mailing Address

Email Address
YouTube Channel
Instagram
Facebook
Streaming
Website
Blog
Birthday or important date(s):

How we met:

Favorite Stitching Things:

Fun Friend Facts:

Name
Social Media Handle
Mailing Address

Email Address
YouTube Channel
Instagram
Facebook
Streaming
Website
Blog
Birthday or important date(s):

How we met:

Favorite Stitching Things:

Fun Friend Facts:

Name
Social Media Handle
Mailing Address

Email Address
YouTube Channel
Instagram
Facebook
Streaming
Website
Blog
Birthday or important date(s):

How we met:

Favorite Stitching Things:

Fun Friend Facts:

Name
Social Media Handle
Mailing Address

Email Address
YouTube Channel
Instagram
Facebook
Streaming
Website
Blog
Birthday or important date(s):

How we met:

Favorite Stitching Things:

Fun Friend Facts:

Name
Social Media Handle
Mailing Address

Email Address
YouTube Channel
Instagram
Facebook
Streaming
Website
Blog
Birthday or important date(s):

How we met:

Favorite Stitching Things:

Fun Friend Facts:

Name
Social Media Handle
Mailing Address

Email Address
YouTube Channel
Instagram
Facebook
Streaming
Website
Blog
Birthday or important date(s):

How we met:

Favorite Stitching Things:

Fun Friend Facts:

Name

Social Media Handle

Mailing Address

Email Address

YouTube Channel

Instagram

Facebook

Streaming

Website

Blog

Birthday or important date(s):

How we met:

Favorite Stitching Things:

Fun Friend Facts:

Name

Social Media Handle

Mailing Address

Email Address

YouTube Channel

Instagram

Facebook

Streaming

Website

Blog

Birthday or important date(s):

How we met:

Favorite Stitching Things:

Fun Friend Facts:

Name
Social Media Handle
Mailing Address

Email Address
YouTube Channel
Instagram
Facebook
Streaming
Website
Blog
Birthday or important date(s):

How we met:

Favorite Stitching Things:

Fun Friend Facts:

Name
Social Media Handle
Mailing Address

Email Address
YouTube Channel
Instagram
Facebook
Streaming
Website
Blog
Birthday or important date(s):

How we met:

Favorite Stitching Things:

Fun Friend Facts:

Name

Social Media Handle

Mailing Address

Email Address

YouTube Channel

Instagram

Facebook

Streaming

Website

Blog

Birthday or important date(s):

How we met:

Favorite Stitching Things:

Fun Friend Facts:

Name

Social Media Handle

Mailing Address

Email Address

YouTube Channel

Instagram

Facebook

Streaming

Website

Blog

Birthday or important date(s):

How we met:

Favorite Stitching Things:

Fun Friend Facts:

Name
Social Media Handle
Mailing Address

Email Address
YouTube Channel
Instagram
Facebook
Streaming
Website
Blog
Birthday or important date(s):

How we met:

Favorite Stitching Things:

Fun Friend Facts:

Name
Social Media Handle
Mailing Address

Email Address
YouTube Channel
Instagram
Facebook
Streaming
Website
Blog
Birthday or important date(s):

How we met:

Favorite Stitching Things:

Fun Friend Facts:

Name
Social Media Handle
Mailing Address

Email Address
YouTube Channel
Instagram
Facebook
Streaming
Website
Blog
Birthday or important date(s):

How we met:

Favorite Stitching Things:

Fun Friend Facts:

Name
Social Media Handle
Mailing Address

Email Address
YouTube Channel
Instagram
Facebook
Streaming
Website
Blog
Birthday or important date(s):

How we met:

Favorite Stitching Things:

Fun Friend Facts:

Name
Social Media Handle
Mailing Address

Email Address
YouTube Channel
Instagram
Facebook
Streaming
Website
Blog
Birthday or important date(s):

How we met:

Favorite Stitching Things:

Fun Friend Facts:

Name
Social Media Handle
Mailing Address

Email Address
YouTube Channel
Instagram
Facebook
Streaming
Website
Blog
Birthday or important date(s):

How we met:

Favorite Stitching Things:

Fun Friend Facts:

Name
Social Media Handle
Mailing Address

Email Address
YouTube Channel
Instagram
Facebook
Streaming
Website
Blog
Birthday or important date(s):

How we met:

Favorite Stitching Things:

Fun Friend Facts:

Name
Social Media Handle
Mailing Address

Email Address
YouTube Channel
Instagram
Facebook
Streaming
Website
Blog
Birthday or important date(s):

How we met:

Favorite Stitching Things:

Fun Friend Facts:

Name
Social Media Handle
Mailing Address

Email Address
YouTube Channel
Instagram
Facebook
Streaming
Website
Blog
Birthday or important date(s):

How we met:

Favorite Stitching Things:

Fun Friend Facts:

Name
Social Media Handle
Mailing Address

Email Address
YouTube Channel
Instagram
Facebook
Streaming
Website
Blog
Birthday or important date(s):

How we met:

Favorite Stitching Things:

Fun Friend Facts:

Name

Social Media Handle

Mailing Address

Email Address

YouTube Channel

Instagram

Facebook

Streaming

Website

Blog

Birthday or important date(s):

How we met:

Favorite Stitching Things:

Fun Friend Facts:

Name

Social Media Handle

Mailing Address

Email Address

YouTube Channel

Instagram

Facebook

Streaming

Website

Blog

Birthday or important date(s):

How we met:

Favorite Stitching Things:

Fun Friend Facts:

Name
Social Media Handle
Mailing Address

Email Address
YouTube Channel
Instagram
Facebook
Streaming
Website
Blog
Birthday or important date(s):

How we met:

Favorite Stitching Things:

Fun Friend Facts:

Name
Social Media Handle
Mailing Address

Email Address
YouTube Channel
Instagram
Facebook
Streaming
Website
Blog
Birthday or important date(s):

How we met:

Favorite Stitching Things:

Fun Friend Facts:

Name

Social Media Handle

Mailing Address

Email Address

YouTube Channel

Instagram

Facebook

Streaming

Website

Blog

Birthday or important date(s):

How we met:

Favorite Stitching Things:

Fun Friend Facts:

Name

Social Media Handle

Mailing Address

Email Address

YouTube Channel

Instagram

Facebook

Streaming

Website

Blog

Birthday or important date(s):

How we met:

Favorite Stitching Things:

Fun Friend Facts:

Name
Social Media Handle
Mailing Address

Email Address
YouTube Channel
Instagram
Facebook
Streaming
Website
Blog
Birthday or important date(s):

How we met:

Favorite Stitching Things:

Fun Friend Facts:

Name
Social Media Handle
Mailing Address

Email Address
YouTube Channel
Instagram
Facebook
Streaming
Website
Blog
Birthday or important date(s):

How we met:

Favorite Stitching Things:

Fun Friend Facts:

Name

Social Media Handle

Mailing Address

Email Address

YouTube Channel

Instagram

Facebook

Streaming

Website

Blog

Birthday or important date(s):

How we met:

Favorite Stitching Things:

Fun Friend Facts:

Name

Social Media Handle

Mailing Address

Email Address

YouTube Channel

Instagram

Facebook

Streaming

Website

Blog

Birthday or important date(s):

How we met:

Favorite Stitching Things:

Fun Friend Facts:

Name
Social Media Handle
Mailing Address

Email Address
YouTube Channel
Instagram
Facebook
Streaming
Website
Blog
Birthday or important date(s):

How we met:

Favorite Stitching Things:

Fun Friend Facts:

Name
Social Media Handle
Mailing Address

Email Address
YouTube Channel
Instagram
Facebook
Streaming
Website
Blog
Birthday or important date(s):

How we met:

Favorite Stitching Things:

Fun Friend Facts:

Name
Social Media Handle
Mailing Address

Email Address
YouTube Channel
Instagram
Facebook
Streaming
Website
Blog
Birthday or important date(s):

How we met:

Favorite Stitching Things:

Fun Friend Facts:

Name
Social Media Handle
Mailing Address

Email Address
YouTube Channel
Instagram
Facebook
Streaming
Website
Blog
Birthday or important date(s):

How we met:

Favorite Stitching Things:

Fun Friend Facts:

Name
Social Media Handle
Mailing Address

Email Address
YouTube Channel
Instagram
Facebook
Streaming
Website
Blog
Birthday or important date(s):

How we met:

Favorite Stitching Things:

Fun Friend Facts:

Name
Social Media Handle
Mailing Address

Email Address
YouTube Channel
Instagram
Facebook
Streaming
Website
Blog
Birthday or important date(s):

How we met:

Favorite Stitching Things:

Fun Friend Facts:

Name

Social Media Handle

Mailing Address

Email Address

YouTube Channel

Instagram

Facebook

Streaming

Website

Blog

Birthday or important date(s):

How we met:

Favorite Stitching Things:

Fun Friend Facts:

Name

Social Media Handle

Mailing Address

Email Address

YouTube Channel

Instagram

Facebook

Streaming

Website

Blog

Birthday or important date(s):

How we met:

Favorite Stitching Things:

Fun Friend Facts:

Name
Social Media Handle
Mailing Address

Email Address
YouTube Channel
Instagram
Facebook
Streaming
Website
Blog
Birthday or important date(s):

How we met:

Favorite Stitching Things:

Fun Friend Facts:

Name
Social Media Handle
Mailing Address

Email Address
YouTube Channel
Instagram
Facebook
Streaming
Website
Blog
Birthday or important date(s):

How we met:

Favorite Stitching Things:

Fun Friend Facts:

Name
Social Media Handle
Mailing Address

Email Address
YouTube Channel
Instagram
Facebook
Streaming
Website
Blog
Birthday or important date(s):

How we met:

Favorite Stitching Things:

Fun Friend Facts:

Name
Social Media Handle
Mailing Address

Email Address
YouTube Channel
Instagram
Facebook
Streaming
Website
Blog
Birthday or important date(s):

How we met:

Favorite Stitching Things:

Fun Friend Facts:

Name
Social Media Handle
Mailing Address

Email Address
YouTube Channel
Instagram
Facebook
Streaming
Website
Blog
Birthday or important date(s):

How we met:

Favorite Stitching Things:

Fun Friend Facts:

Name
Social Media Handle
Mailing Address

Email Address
YouTube Channel
Instagram
Facebook
Streaming
Website
Blog
Birthday or important date(s):

How we met:

Favorite Stitching Things:

Fun Friend Facts:

Name
Social Media Handle
Mailing Address

Email Address
YouTube Channel
Instagram
Facebook
Streaming
Website
Blog
Birthday or important date(s):

How we met:

Favorite Stitching Things:

Fun Friend Facts:

Name
Social Media Handle
Mailing Address

Email Address
YouTube Channel
Instagram
Facebook
Streaming
Website
Blog
Birthday or important date(s):

How we met:

Favorite Stitching Things:

Fun Friend Facts:

Name
Social Media Handle
Mailing Address

Email Address
YouTube Channel
Instagram
Facebook
Streaming
Website
Blog
Birthday or important date(s):

How we met:

Favorite Stitching Things:

Fun Friend Facts:

Name
Social Media Handle
Mailing Address

Email Address
YouTube Channel
Instagram
Facebook
Streaming
Website
Blog
Birthday or important date(s):

How we met:

Favorite Stitching Things:

Fun Friend Facts:

Name

Social Media Handle

Mailing Address

Email Address

YouTube Channel

Instagram

Facebook

Streaming

Website

Blog

Birthday or important date(s):

How we met:

Favorite Stitching Things:

Fun Friend Facts:

Name

Social Media Handle

Mailing Address

Email Address

YouTube Channel

Instagram

Facebook

Streaming

Website

Blog

Birthday or important date(s):

How we met:

Favorite Stitching Things:

Fun Friend Facts:

Name
Social Media Handle
Mailing Address

Email Address
YouTube Channel
Instagram
Facebook
Streaming
Website
Blog
Birthday or important date(s):

How we met:

Favorite Stitching Things:

Fun Friend Facts:

Name
Social Media Handle
Mailing Address

Email Address
YouTube Channel
Instagram
Facebook
Streaming
Website
Blog
Birthday or important date(s):

How we met:

Favorite Stitching Things:

Fun Friend Facts:

Name
Social Media Handle
Mailing Address

Email Address
YouTube Channel
Instagram
Facebook
Streaming
Website
Blog
Birthday or important date(s):

How we met:

Favorite Stitching Things:

Fun Friend Facts:

Name
Social Media Handle
Mailing Address

Email Address
YouTube Channel
Instagram
Facebook
Streaming
Website
Blog
Birthday or important date(s):

How we met:

Favorite Stitching Things:

Fun Friend Facts:

Name

Social Media Handle

Mailing Address

Email Address

YouTube Channel

Instagram

Facebook

Streaming

Website

Blog

Birthday or important date(s):

How we met:

Favorite Stitching Things:

Fun Friend Facts:

Name

Social Media Handle

Mailing Address

Email Address

YouTube Channel

Instagram

Facebook

Streaming

Website

Blog

Birthday or important date(s):

How we met:

Favorite Stitching Things:

Fun Friend Facts:

Name

Social Media Handle

Mailing Address

Email Address

YouTube Channel

Instagram

Facebook

Streaming

Website

Blog

Birthday or important date(s):

How we met:

Favorite Stitching Things:

Fun Friend Facts:

Name

Social Media Handle

Mailing Address

Email Address

YouTube Channel

Instagram

Facebook

Streaming

Website

Blog

Birthday or important date(s):

How we met:

Favorite Stitching Things:

Fun Friend Facts:

Name
Social Media Handle
Mailing Address

Email Address
YouTube Channel
Instagram
Facebook
Streaming
Website
Blog
Birthday or important date(s):

How we met:

Favorite Stitching Things:

Fun Friend Facts:

Name
Social Media Handle
Mailing Address

Email Address
YouTube Channel
Instagram
Facebook
Streaming
Website
Blog
Birthday or important date(s):

How we met:

Favorite Stitching Things:

Fun Friend Facts:

Name

Social Media Handle

Mailing Address

Email Address

YouTube Channel

Instagram

Facebook

Streaming

Website

Blog

Birthday or important date(s):

How we met:

Favorite Stitching Things:

Fun Friend Facts:

Name

Social Media Handle

Mailing Address

Email Address

YouTube Channel

Instagram

Facebook

Streaming

Website

Blog

Birthday or important date(s):

How we met:

Favorite Stitching Things:

Fun Friend Facts:

Name
Social Media Handle
Mailing Address

Email Address
YouTube Channel
Instagram
Facebook
Streaming
Website
Blog
Birthday or important date(s):

How we met:

Favorite Stitching Things:

Fun Friend Facts:

Name
Social Media Handle
Mailing Address

Email Address
YouTube Channel
Instagram
Facebook
Streaming
Website
Blog
Birthday or important date(s):

How we met:

Favorite Stitching Things:

Fun Friend Facts:

Name
Social Media Handle
Mailing Address

Email Address
YouTube Channel
Instagram
Facebook
Streaming
Website
Blog
Birthday or important date(s):

How we met:

Favorite Stitching Things:

Fun Friend Facts:

Name
Social Media Handle
Mailing Address

Email Address
YouTube Channel
Instagram
Facebook
Streaming
Website
Blog
Birthday or important date(s):

How we met:

Favorite Stitching Things:

Fun Friend Facts:

Name
Social Media Handle
Mailing Address

Email Address
YouTube Channel
Instagram
Facebook
Streaming
Website
Blog
Birthday or important date(s):

How we met:

Favorite Stitching Things:

Fun Friend Facts:

Name
Social Media Handle
Mailing Address

Email Address
YouTube Channel
Instagram
Facebook
Streaming
Website
Blog
Birthday or important date(s):

How we met:

Favorite Stitching Things:

Fun Friend Facts:

Name

Social Media Handle

Mailing Address

Email Address

YouTube Channel

Instagram

Facebook

Streaming

Website

Blog

Birthday or important date(s):

How we met:

Favorite Stitching Things:

Fun Friend Facts:

Name

Social Media Handle

Mailing Address

Email Address

YouTube Channel

Instagram

Facebook

Streaming

Website

Blog

Birthday or important date(s):

How we met:

Favorite Stitching Things:

Fun Friend Facts:

Name
Social Media Handle
Mailing Address

Email Address
YouTube Channel
Instagram
Facebook
Streaming
Website
Blog
Birthday or important date(s):

How we met:

Favorite Stitching Things:

Fun Friend Facts:

Name
Social Media Handle
Mailing Address

Email Address
YouTube Channel
Instagram
Facebook
Streaming
Website
Blog
Birthday or important date(s):

How we met:

Favorite Stitching Things:

Fun Friend Facts:

Name

Social Media Handle

Mailing Address

Email Address

YouTube Channel

Instagram

Facebook

Streaming

Website

Blog

Birthday or important date(s):

How we met:

Favorite Stitching Things:

Fun Friend Facts:

Name

Social Media Handle

Mailing Address

Email Address

YouTube Channel

Instagram

Facebook

Streaming

Website

Blog

Birthday or important date(s):

How we met:

Favorite Stitching Things:

Fun Friend Facts:

Name
Social Media Handle
Mailing Address

Email Address
YouTube Channel
Instagram
Facebook
Streaming
Website
Blog
Birthday or important date(s):

How we met:

Favorite Stitching Things:

Fun Friend Facts:

Name
Social Media Handle
Mailing Address

Email Address
YouTube Channel
Instagram
Facebook
Streaming
Website
Blog
Birthday or important date(s):

How we met:

Favorite Stitching Things:

Fun Friend Facts:

Name _____

Social Media Handle _____

Mailing Address _____

_____

Email Address _____

YouTube Channel _____

Instagram _____

Facebook _____

Streaming _____

Website _____

Blog _____

Birthday or important date(s): _____

_____

How we met: _____

_____

Favorite Stitching Things: _____

_____

_____

Fun Friend Facts: _____

_____

_____

Name _____

Social Media Handle _____

Mailing Address _____

_____

Email Address _____

YouTube Channel _____

Instagram _____

Facebook _____

Streaming _____

Website _____

Blog _____

Birthday or important date(s): _____

_____

How we met: _____

_____

Favorite Stitching Things: _____

_____

_____

Fun Friend Facts: _____

_____

_____

Name
Social Media Handle
Mailing Address

Email Address
YouTube Channel
Instagram
Facebook
Streaming
Website
Blog
Birthday or important date(s):

How we met:

Favorite Stitching Things:

Fun Friend Facts:

Name
Social Media Handle
Mailing Address

Email Address
YouTube Channel
Instagram
Facebook
Streaming
Website
Blog
Birthday or important date(s):

How we met:

Favorite Stitching Things:

Fun Friend Facts:

Name

Social Media Handle

Mailing Address

Email Address

YouTube Channel

Instagram

Facebook

Streaming

Website

Blog

Birthday or important date(s):

How we met:

Favorite Stitching Things:

Fun Friend Facts:

Name

Social Media Handle

Mailing Address

Email Address

YouTube Channel

Instagram

Facebook

Streaming

Website

Blog

Birthday or important date(s):

How we met:

Favorite Stitching Things:

Fun Friend Facts:

Name
Social Media Handle
Mailing Address

Email Address
YouTube Channel
Instagram
Facebook
Streaming
Website
Blog
Birthday or important date(s):

How we met:

Favorite Stitching Things:

Fun Friend Facts:

Name
Social Media Handle
Mailing Address

Email Address
YouTube Channel
Instagram
Facebook
Streaming
Website
Blog
Birthday or important date(s):

How we met:

Favorite Stitching Things:

Fun Friend Facts:

Name

Social Media Handle

Mailing Address

Email Address

YouTube Channel

Instagram

Facebook

Streaming

Website

Blog

Birthday or important date(s):

How we met:

Favorite Stitching Things:

Fun Friend Facts:

Name

Social Media Handle

Mailing Address

Email Address

YouTube Channel

Instagram

Facebook

Streaming

Website

Blog

Birthday or important date(s):

How we met:

Favorite Stitching Things:

Fun Friend Facts:

Name
Social Media Handle
Mailing Address

Email Address
YouTube Channel
Instagram
Facebook
Streaming
Website
Blog
Birthday or important date(s):

How we met:

Favorite Stitching Things:

Fun Friend Facts:

Name
Social Media Handle
Mailing Address

Email Address
YouTube Channel
Instagram
Facebook
Streaming
Website
Blog
Birthday or important date(s):

How we met:

Favorite Stitching Things:

Fun Friend Facts:

Name

Social Media Handle

Mailing Address

Email Address

YouTube Channel

Instagram

Facebook

Streaming

Website

Blog

Birthday or important date(s):

How we met:

Favorite Stitching Things:

Fun Friend Facts:

Name

Social Media Handle

Mailing Address

Email Address

YouTube Channel

Instagram

Facebook

Streaming

Website

Blog

Birthday or important date(s):

How we met:

Favorite Stitching Things:

Fun Friend Facts:

Name
Social Media Handle
Mailing Address

Email Address
YouTube Channel
Instagram
Facebook
Streaming
Website
Blog
Birthday or important date(s):

How we met:

Favorite Stitching Things:

Fun Friend Facts:

Name
Social Media Handle
Mailing Address

Email Address
YouTube Channel
Instagram
Facebook
Streaming
Website
Blog
Birthday or important date(s):

How we met:

Favorite Stitching Things:

Fun Friend Facts:

Name

Social Media Handle

Mailing Address

Email Address

YouTube Channel

Instagram

Facebook

Streaming

Website

Blog

Birthday or important date(s):

How we met:

Favorite Stitching Things:

Fun Friend Facts:

Name

Social Media Handle

Mailing Address

Email Address

YouTube Channel

Instagram

Facebook

Streaming

Website

Blog

Birthday or important date(s):

How we met:

Favorite Stitching Things:

Fun Friend Facts:

Name
Social Media Handle
Mailing Address

Email Address
YouTube Channel
Instagram
Facebook
Streaming
Website
Blog
Birthday or important date(s):

How we met:

Favorite Stitching Things:

Fun Friend Facts:

Name
Social Media Handle
Mailing Address

Email Address
YouTube Channel
Instagram
Facebook
Streaming
Website
Blog
Birthday or important date(s):

How we met:

Favorite Stitching Things:

Fun Friend Facts:

Name
Social Media Handle
Mailing Address

Email Address
YouTube Channel
Instagram
Facebook
Streaming
Website
Blog
Birthday or important date(s):

How we met:

Favorite Stitching Things:

Fun Friend Facts:

Name
Social Media Handle
Mailing Address

Email Address
YouTube Channel
Instagram
Facebook
Streaming
Website
Blog
Birthday or important date(s):

How we met:

Favorite Stitching Things:

Fun Friend Facts:

Name
Social Media Handle
Mailing Address

Email Address
YouTube Channel
Instagram
Facebook
Streaming
Website
Blog
Birthday or important date(s):

How we met:

Favorite Stitching Things:

Fun Friend Facts:

Name
Social Media Handle
Mailing Address

Email Address
YouTube Channel
Instagram
Facebook
Streaming
Website
Blog
Birthday or important date(s):

How we met:

Favorite Stitching Things:

Fun Friend Facts:

Name

Social Media Handle

Mailing Address

Email Address

YouTube Channel

Instagram

Facebook

Streaming

Website

Blog

Birthday or important date(s):

How we met:

Favorite Stitching Things:

Fun Friend Facts:

Name

Social Media Handle

Mailing Address

Email Address

YouTube Channel

Instagram

Facebook

Streaming

Website

Blog

Birthday or important date(s):

How we met:

Favorite Stitching Things:

Fun Friend Facts:

Name
Social Media Handle
Mailing Address

Email Address
YouTube Channel
Instagram
Facebook
Streaming
Website
Blog
Birthday or important date(s):

How we met:

Favorite Stitching Things:

Fun Friend Facts:

Name
Social Media Handle
Mailing Address

Email Address
YouTube Channel
Instagram
Facebook
Streaming
Website
Blog
Birthday or important date(s):

How we met:

Favorite Stitching Things:

Fun Friend Facts:

Name

Social Media Handle

Mailing Address

Email Address

YouTube Channel

Instagram

Facebook

Streaming

Website

Blog

Birthday or important date(s):

How we met:

Favorite Stitching Things:

Fun Friend Facts:

Name

Social Media Handle

Mailing Address

Email Address

YouTube Channel

Instagram

Facebook

Streaming

Website

Blog

Birthday or important date(s):

How we met:

Favorite Stitching Things:

Fun Friend Facts:

Name
Social Media Handle
Mailing Address

Email Address
YouTube Channel
Instagram
Facebook
Streaming
Website
Blog
Birthday or important date(s):

How we met:

Favorite Stitching Things:

Fun Friend Facts:

Name
Social Media Handle
Mailing Address

Email Address
YouTube Channel
Instagram
Facebook
Streaming
Website
Blog
Birthday or important date(s):

How we met:

Favorite Stitching Things:

Fun Friend Facts:

Name
Social Media Handle
Mailing Address

Email Address
YouTube Channel
Instagram
Facebook
Streaming
Website
Blog
Birthday or important date(s):

How we met:

Favorite Stitching Things:

Fun Friend Facts:

Name
Social Media Handle
Mailing Address

Email Address
YouTube Channel
Instagram
Facebook
Streaming
Website
Blog
Birthday or important date(s):

How we met:

Favorite Stitching Things:

Fun Friend Facts:

Name
Social Media Handle
Mailing Address

Email Address
YouTube Channel
Instagram
Facebook
Streaming
Website
Blog
Birthday or important date(s):

How we met:

Favorite Stitching Things:

Fun Friend Facts:

Name
Social Media Handle
Mailing Address

Email Address
YouTube Channel
Instagram
Facebook
Streaming
Website
Blog
Birthday or important date(s):

How we met:

Favorite Stitching Things:

Fun Friend Facts:

Name

Social Media Handle

Mailing Address

Email Address

YouTube Channel

Instagram

Facebook

Streaming

Website

Blog

Birthday or important date(s):

How we met:

Favorite Stitching Things:

Fun Friend Facts:

Name

Social Media Handle

Mailing Address

Email Address

YouTube Channel

Instagram

Facebook

Streaming

Website

Blog

Birthday or important date(s):

How we met:

Favorite Stitching Things:

Fun Friend Facts:

Name
Social Media Handle
Mailing Address

Email Address
YouTube Channel
Instagram
Facebook
Streaming
Website
Blog
Birthday or important date(s):

How we met:

Favorite Stitching Things:

Fun Friend Facts:

Name
Social Media Handle
Mailing Address

Email Address
YouTube Channel
Instagram
Facebook
Streaming
Website
Blog
Birthday or important date(s):

How we met:

Favorite Stitching Things:

Fun Friend Facts:

Name

Social Media Handle

Mailing Address

Email Address

YouTube Channel

Instagram

Facebook

Streaming

Website

Blog

Birthday or important date(s):

How we met:

Favorite Stitching Things:

Fun Friend Facts:

Name

Social Media Handle

Mailing Address

Email Address

YouTube Channel

Instagram

Facebook

Streaming

Website

Blog

Birthday or important date(s):

How we met:

Favorite Stitching Things:

Fun Friend Facts:

Name
Social Media Handle
Mailing Address

Email Address
YouTube Channel
Instagram
Facebook
Streaming
Website
Blog
Birthday or important date(s):

How we met:

Favorite Stitching Things:

Fun Friend Facts:

Name
Social Media Handle
Mailing Address

Email Address
YouTube Channel
Instagram
Facebook
Streaming
Website
Blog
Birthday or important date(s):

How we met:

Favorite Stitching Things:

Fun Friend Facts:

Name
Social Media Handle
Mailing Address

Email Address
YouTube Channel
Instagram
Facebook
Streaming
Website
Blog
Birthday or important date(s):

How we met:

Favorite Stitching Things:

Fun Friend Facts:

Name
Social Media Handle
Mailing Address

Email Address
YouTube Channel
Instagram
Facebook
Streaming
Website
Blog
Birthday or important date(s):

How we met:

Favorite Stitching Things:

Fun Friend Facts:

Made in the USA
Columbia, SC
20 January 2023

10773231R00074